Canada's
LAND & PEOPLE

QUEBEC

Rennay Craats

Weigl

CALGARY
www.weigl.com

Published by Weigl Educational Publishers Limited
6325 10 Street SE
Calgary, Alberta   T2H 2Z9

Website: www.weigl.com
Copyright ©2008 Weigl Educational Publishers Limited

Library and Archives Canada Cataloguing in Publication

Craats, Rennay, 1973-
     Quebec / Rennay Craats.

(Canada's land and people)
Includes index.
ISBN 978-1-55388-357-9 (bound)
ISBN 978-1-55388-358-6 (pbk.)

     1. Québec (Province)--Juvenile literature. I. Title. II. Series.
FC2911.2.C73185 2007   j971.4   C2007-902202-2

Printed in the United States of America
1 2 3 4 5 6 7 8 9 0 11 10 09 08 07

Every reasonable effort has been made to trace ownership and to obtain permission to reprint copyright material. The publishers would be pleased to have any errors or omissions brought to their attention so that they may be corrected in subsequent printings.

We acknowledge the financial support of the Government of Canada through the Book Publishing Industry Development Program (BPIDP) for our publishing activities.

Photograph credits: Gouvernement du Québec: page 4 bottom left; Quebec Capitales: page 19 middle left.

Project Coordinator
Heather C. Hudak

Design
Terry Paulhus

Contents

About Quebec

Quebec is Canada's largest province in area. The province covers 1,540,680 square kilometres of land.

Most people in Quebec speak French. Schools teach students in French. Street signs are written in French and English.

Quebec joined Confederation on July 1, 1867. The province's name comes from the Algonquian word *kebek*. It means "where the river narrows." The word described the Saint Lawrence River near today's Quebec City.

The **fleur-de-lis** is a symbol of France. *Fleur* means flower. *Lis* means lily. The symbol appears on many of Quebec's official emblems, such as the coat of arms and the flag.

ABOUT THE FLAG

Quebec became the first Canadian province to adopt an official flag in 1948. It shows a white cross on a blue field to honour past French military flags. Four fleurs-de-lis represent the kings of France and the early French settlers. In 1999, Quebec made the provincial flag its official emblem.

LEGEND

Yukon
Northwest Territories
Nunavut
British Columbia
Alberta
Saskatchewan
Manitoba
Ontario
Quebec
Newfoundland & Labrador
New Brunswick
Prince Edward Island
Nova Scotia

ACTION Draw a coat of arms for your family. Most coats of arms look like a shield decorated with symbols, such as the fleur-de-lis. Use colors and symbols that have special meaning to your family. Write about your coat of arms. Explain why you chose those symbols and colors.

Places to Visit in Quebec

There are many places to see in Quebec. This map shows just a few. What places do you think are special in Quebec? Can you find where they would be on the map?

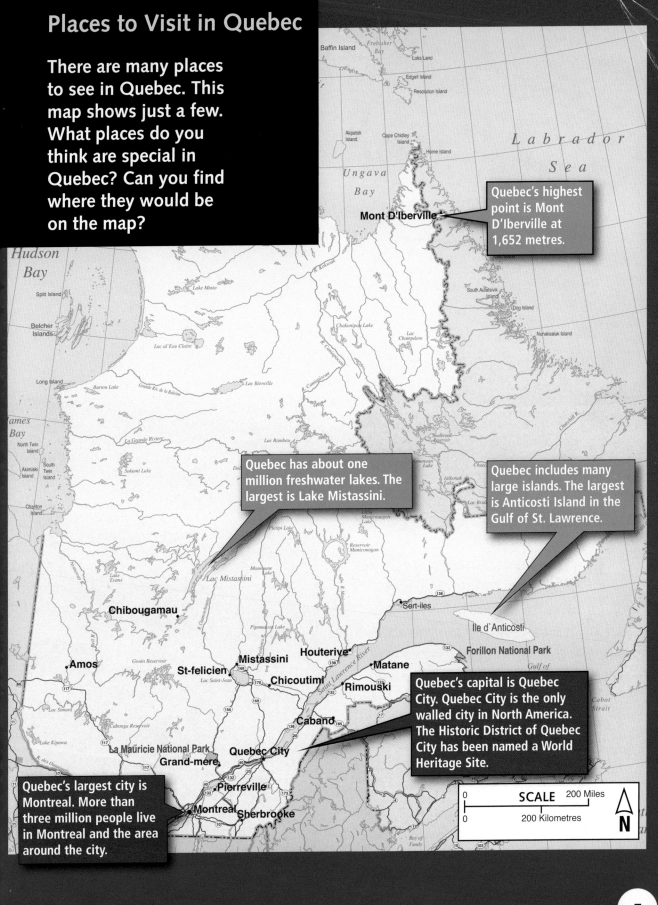

Quebec's highest point is Mont D'Iberville at 1,652 metres.

Quebec has about one million freshwater lakes. The largest is Lake Mistassini.

Quebec includes many large islands. The largest is Anticosti Island in the Gulf of St. Lawrence.

Quebec's capital is Quebec City. Quebec City is the only walled city in North America. The Historic District of Quebec City has been named a World Heritage Site.

Quebec's largest city is Montreal. More than three million people live in Montreal and the area around the city.

SCALE
0   200 Miles
0   200 Kilometres
N

Beautiful Landscapes

Quebec is nicknamed *la belle province*. In English, this means "beautiful province." **Glaciers** in Quebec melted long ago. They left behind many lakes and rivers. Quebec is mostly covered by the rocky Canadian Shield. The province has the fertile Saint Lawrence Lowlands and the hilly Appalachian Highlands. Cold northern winds crash into warm southern winds over Quebec. This makes heavy rain and snow. The province has long, cold winters and hot, humid summers.

Quebec's far northern Canadian Shield has a **tundra**, or cold desert. Rocks found in the Canadian Shield are among the oldest in the world.

Quebec's Laurentian Highlands mark the southern edge of the Canadian Shield. Thick forests cover much of the hilly land.

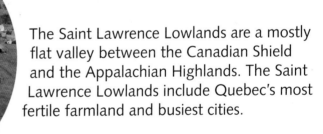

The Saint Lawrence Lowlands are a mostly flat valley between the Canadian Shield and the Appalachian Highlands. The Saint Lawrence Lowlands include Quebec's most fertile farmland and busiest cities.

Quebec's Appalachian Highlands lie on the southern side of the Saint Lawrence River. The **Appalachian Range** stretches from the Gaspé Peninsula to the Gulf of Mexico in the United States.

Fur, Feathers, and Flowers

Forests cover much of Quebec. Colourful wildflowers blossom from spring to fall. Salmon, northern pike, and many other fish live in the province's rivers and lakes. The province is home to about 300 bird species, too. Quebec's many mammals range in size. Some are small, such as the mink, rabbit, otter, and beaver. Other mammals are large, such as the polar bear, wolf, caribou, moose, white-tailed deer, and beluga whale. About 500 beluga whales live in the Gulf of Saint Lawrence. Other whales and seals swim in the waters off Quebec's northern coast.

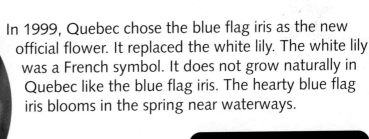

In 1999, Quebec chose the blue flag iris as the new official flower. It replaced the white lily. The white lily was a French symbol. It does not grow naturally in Quebec like the blue flag iris. The hearty blue flag iris blooms in the spring near waterways.

The snowy owl was named Quebec's provincial bird in 1987. This large bird measures about 53 to 65 centimetres tall. Its body temperature stays at about 40 degrees Celsius, even with air temperatures at –50° Celsius.

The yellow birch tree is the official tree of Quebec. This tree has always been important to Quebec's people. Settlers used this type of tree for furniture. Today, the yellow birch is important for lumber and for woodland **habitats**.

In 1998, Quebec citizens chose the white admiral butterfly as a provincial symbol. This butterfly lives near the province's woodland areas.

Rich in Resources

Early settlers fished, farmed, and traded furs. Later, Quebec's forestry and mining industries became more important. Forest and mineral resources are still important today. Manufacturing, tourism, education, and health care lead the province's economy. Quebec has more fresh water than any other province. The water is used to make electricity. The province is Canada's largest producer of electricity.

Quebec borders the Saint Lawrence River. It is one of the world's major water routes. The Saint Lawrence Seaway links the Atlantic Ocean to the Great Lakes. More than 30 Quebec ports welcome ocean-going vessels.

Montreal has been one of Canada's leading manufacturing centres since the 1800s. Quebec's factories make clothing, food, pulp, and paper. The province produces more than half of all of Canada's parts for airplanes and other flight equipment.

Quebec harvests more than 35 million cubic kilometres of trees each year for lumber, pulp, and paper. Maple trees produce sap that is used to make maple syrup. Quebec produces more than 15 million litres of maple syrup a year. The province supplies most of Canada's maple syrup.

Quebec has many metals, such as gold, zinc, copper, silver, or nickel. Canada's largest gold deposit is in LaRonde. The mine produces about seven million grams of gold each year. In 2001, diamonds were discovered east of Ungava Bay.

Quebec is one of Canada's leading sources for dairy products. About 7,600 Quebec dairy farms produce more than 3 billion litres of milk each year.

Shaped by History

Algonquian, Iroquoian, and Inuit are among the Aboriginal Peoples in Quebec. The Algonquian nations were known for their hunting and fishing skills. They moved between winter and summer camps. The Iroquoians farmed near the Saint Lawrence River Valley. They built homes near their farms. The Inuit lived along the Hudson Bay and Ungava Peninsula. They, too, were strong hunters and fishers. The Inuit used dogsleds for travel. Today, dogsleds are still popular among the Inuit and others living in the snowy North. About 7,500 Inuit live in villages along the coasts of the Ungava Bay and Hudson Bay. More than 50,000 Aboriginal Peoples live in Quebec. Some live on the many **reserves** across the province.

French explorer Jacques Cartier reached the Gaspé Peninsula in 1534. He claimed the land for France. Cartier thought he had found gold and diamonds. Back in France, Cartier learned his riches were worthless iron pyrite, or "fool's gold", and sparkly **quartz**. Major deposits of gold and diamonds were found in Quebec in the 1900s and 2000s.

French fishers and fur traders arrived in "New France" in the 1580s. They stayed during the warm seasons. The fishers and traders returned to France for the winters. In 1608, Samuel de Champlain built a **trading post** on the Saint Lawrence River. He hoped to attract French settlers to New France. Fewer than 10,000 French settlers moved to the colony between 1608 and 1763. Today, about five million people in Quebec trace their family history to early French settlers.

De passage ou pour un séjour prolongé, HÉROUXVILLE vous accueille!

Quebec was a French colony until Great Britain won control in 1763. In 1791, Great Britain made the Quebec area a separate region called Lower Canada or Canada East. Most people in Lower Canada spoke French.

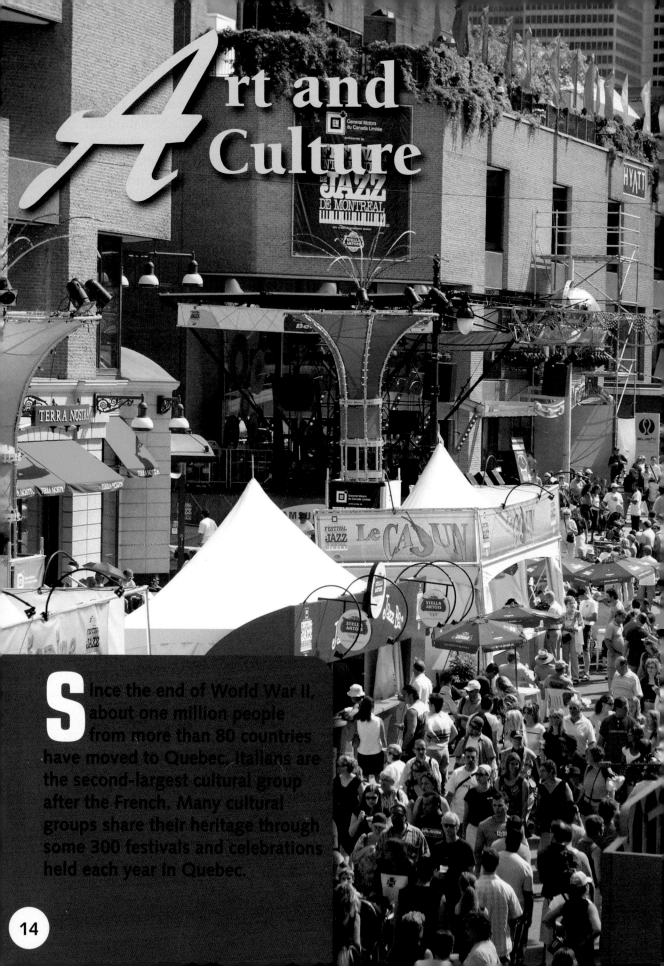

Art and Culture

Since the end of World War II, about one million people from more than 80 countries have moved to Quebec. Italians are the second-largest cultural group after the French. Many cultural groups share their heritage through some 300 festivals and celebrations held each year in Quebec.

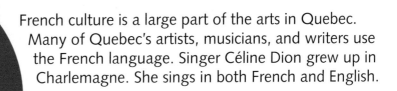

French culture is a large part of the arts in Quebec. Many of Quebec's artists, musicians, and writers use the French language. Singer Céline Dion grew up in Charlemagne. She sings in both French and English.

Montreal has become Quebec's centre for the arts. It is the largest French-speaking city in the world after Paris, France. Many performing arts companies are located in Montreal, such as Cirque du Soleil.

Quebec has many universities and colleges. McGill University was founded in Montreal in 1821. It is Canada's oldest university.

The Place-Royale at Quebec City has been called "the birthplace of French America." The site honours Samuel de Champlain's trading post. It was built there about 400 years ago.

Points of Interest

Three national parks are located in Quebec. Each features a unique look at Quebec's vast and varied wilderness areas. The province has 16 wildlife reserves and 22 provincial parks. The provincial park system includes more than 80,000 square kilometres of outdoor places to explore. Across Quebec, many places celebrate nature and honour history. About 180 places in Quebec have been named national historic sites.

La Mauricie National Park in the Laurentian mountains was created in 1970 to protect the area's wilderness and animals. Hilly forests lead to quiet lakes where limited fishing for brook trout is allowed.

Wind and waves have created more than 1,000 rocky islands and **outcrops** near Quebec's north shore. The Gulf of Saint Lawrence Mingan Archipelago became a national park reserve in 1984.

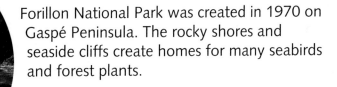

Forillon National Park was created in 1970 on Gaspé Peninsula. The rocky shores and seaside cliffs create homes for many seabirds and forest plants.

The Montmorency Falls near Quebec City are 83 metres high. About 35,000 litres of water flow over the falls every second. The Montmorency Falls are higher than Niagara Falls.

A major bird migration route passes over the Cap-Tourmente National Wildlife Area. Nearly one million greater snow geese flock to the Cap-Tourmente saltwater marsh every year.

Sports and Activities

The first Stanley Cup playoff hockey game took place in Montreal on March 22, 1894. The Stanley Cup became part of the National Hockey League (NHL) in 1916. Since then, the Montreal Canadiens hockey team has won the Stanley Cup 24 times. Four seasons of sports and outdoor activities add to a healthy lifestyle in Quebec. Many schools and local recreation centres encourage **amateur** athletes in almost all modern sports.

Montreal's downtown cricket grounds hosted the first recorded football game ever played in North America on October 10, 1868. Today, the Montreal Alouettes play in the Canadian Football League at the Percival Molson Memorial Stadium near downtown Montreal.

The Quebec Capitales baseball team joined the Canadian American (CanAm) professional league in 1999. The Capitales clinched the CanAm League Championship in 2006.

Racecar driver Jacques Villeneuve from Quebec won the Indianapolis 500 in 1995. Villeneuve has won many other races and championships, including the 1997 Formula One world championship.

In the winter season, snowshoeing, and downhill and cross-country skiing are popular outdoor activities in Quebec. Indoor and outdoor rinks attract hockey and figure skaters of all ages.

What Others Are Saying

Many people have great things to say about Quebec.

"Between these quiet villages and the bustling cities, the visitor discovers the true meaning of these legendary wide open spaces he heard so much about and that made the reputation of Quebec as an exceptional travel destination."

Quebec writer Anne Hébert called Quebec the "original heart" of Canada, "the hardest and deepest kernel."

"To a traveller from the Old World, Canada East may appear like a new country, and its inhabitants like colonists, but to me, coming from New England and being a very green traveler withall,... it appeared as old as Normandy itself, and realized much that I had heard of Europe and the Middle Ages."

"...Quebec is, today and forever, a distinct society, that is free and able to assume [the control of] its destiny and its development."

ACTION Think about the place where you live. Come up with some words to describe your province, city, or community. Are there rolling hills and deep valleys? Can you see trees or lakes? What are some of the features of the land, people, and buildings that make your home special? Use these words to write a paragraph about the place where you live.

Test Your Knowledge

What have you learned about Quebec? Try answering the following questions.

1 What language is most often spoken in Quebec? What other ways is that culture a part of life in Quebec today?

2 What were some of the ways that Aboriginal Peoples found food in Quebec? Visit the library to learn more about how European settlers changed the ways Aboriginal Peoples lived in the 1600s.

3 What types of animals live in Quebec? Look online to learn more about the animals and their habitats. Write a paragraph about your favourite Quebec animal, and draw a picture of it.

Tour Guide Time

Choose one of the many parks in Quebec. Use online information or library books to help you explore the park. Write a paragraph telling a visitor what he or she will experience at the park.

Further Research

Books

To find out more about Quebec and other Canadian provinces and territories, visit your local library. Most libraries have computers that connect to a database for researching information. If you input a key word, you will be provided with a list of books in the library that contain information on that topic. Non-fiction books are arranged numerically, using their call number. Fiction books are organized alphabetically by the author's last name.

Websites

The World Wide Web is a good source of information. Reliable websites usually include government sites, educational sites, and online encyclopedias. Visit the following sites to learn more about Quebec.

Go to the Government of Quebec's website to learn about the province's government, history, and climate.
www.gouv.qc.ca

The Quebec Tour Guide is a travel site that shows things to do and see in the province.
www.quebecweb.com/tourisme/introang

Visit The Parks Canada site. Click "National Parks of Canada" to see a list for each province.
www.pc.gc.ca

Glossary

amateur: to play for fun, not pay or as a job

Appalachian Range: a line of mountains stretching from Quebec to the Gulf of Mexico in eastern North America

fleur-de-lis: a French symbol of the lily

glaciers: huge chunks of ice that move slowly, usually down from mountaintops

habitats: places where an animal or plant naturally lives or grows

outcrops: rocky grounds that are not covered with soil

quartz: a hard, glossy mineral in crystal form

reserves: areas of land set apart, usually by treaty, for First Nations

trading post: a store of a trader, especially in a place far from other stores

tundra: a treeless plain in an arctic region

Index